Uh-Uh, Daughter, DON'T EVEN GO THERE

Minister Patricia S. Hatcher-Jones

TABLE OF CONTENTS

DEDICATION

I dedicate this book to my late mama, Mildred Louise Hatcher, the woman who invested her best wisdom, knowledge, and love into my life, and to my late daddy, Raymond Jewel Hatcher, Sr., the man who would demonstrate to me what being a bona fide father and man is all about. I thank God for you both because, without you, there would be no me. I love you!

"Your job is to speak out on the things that make for solid doctrine."
(Titus 2:1 – MSG)

This book is written for and dedicated to all my little Sistas who are considering going "there." Where is "there"? "There" is the area of false satisfaction and temporary fulfillment where our flesh is lured to, but our spirit cannot rest in peace.

I didn't grow up with sisters. I'm the fifth of six children (all brothers). Everything I experienced was by trial and error. Although many older females were in the neighborhood, none recognized the need to take me under their wings and mentor me. Now that I'm older, I don't consider this as necessarily a bad thing because many of them made poor choices that resulted in adverse circumstances, such as pregnancies out of wedlock, drug addictions, bad marriages, and suicides. I realize now that God protected me from their ungodly counsel. He (God) would be the voice to say, "Uh-uh, daughter, don't even go there!" Sometimes, I took heed to the warnings, but oftentimes, I did not.

God has allowed me to survive my challenges as a young lady on this life's journey. I pray my first-hand experience will prevent some of you from yielding to the temptations that are designed to kill, steal, and destroy you. I pray that by reading this book, you will discover how to listen to the voice of Jesus as He says, "Uh-uh, daughter, don't even go there!" We have been or will be tempted to enter the "there" zone. But be of good cheer because the Lord has a word and hope for you.

BOOK REVIEWS

"My favorite chapters were Chapter 8 - "Don't Fail to Honor your parents and Chapter 9 - "Don't Live with Unforgiveness". The reason I like Chapter 8 is because, to tell you the truth, I don't really honor my parents a lot like I should be doing, and that chapter really spoke to me about honoring my parents and to treat them with respect even though they may make me mad sometimes. I realized, after reading the book, that I should always treat them with respect and honor them. Now, chapter nine was about forgiveness, and when someone gets me mad, I usually never forgive them, but when I read the book, it said if I don't forgive, God won't forgive me. So now I know that I must forgive."

13-year-old from California

"I fell in love with Uh-Uh, Daughter, Don't Even Go There after I read it. My mom wanted me to read the book, but I refused to because I thought it was another book telling her how to discipline me. Me and my mom have been going through some hard times and I felt like she didn't like me, just as you thought about your mom. When she told me to read it, I straight up told her NO. She didn't say anything to me again about the book. Then one day while I was waiting for her in the car while she shopped, I noticed the book and picked it up and was drawn in after reading the first chapter, "Don't Allow Makeup to Create a Different You" spoke to me. Prior to reading the book, I saw myself falling in a trap and I asked God to help me with it. Then He answered my prayer and sent you (well your book - LOL). After reading your book, many of my questions were answered that I couldn't go to my mom with. I can truly see God makes a way for everything. I just had to let you know that this book positively and greatly affected me, and I thank you for it."

16-year-old from Texas

She purchased the book and, after reading it, used chapter 10, "Don't Let the Voice of Suicide Speak," as the foundation for a group discussion with her youth. She testified that the suicide chapter was relevant and timely, and many young girls were helped, encouraged, and inspired by the group discussion. She also used some of the group discussion questions to engage in dialogue with her youth.

A Youth Group Counselor

Uh-Uh, Daughter, Don't Even Go There has blessed not only girls and grown women, but men have also read the book and bought copies for their daughters. A Father from Stockton, CA, called me and requested a copy to give to his teenage daughter after he read Chapter Two, "Don't Let Your Flesh Dictate What You Wear."

A Father from California

"Uh-Uh, Daughter, Don't Even Go There" is equal parts inspiration and seasoned wisdom. Patricia S. Hatcher-Jones motivates and encourages with the word of God and leverages the power of her unique personal testimony as well. Her honest, highly relatable voice makes us completely believe she knows what she speaks. Read it and be blessed.

Ronn Elmore, Psy. D., Author, "How to Love a Black Man

DON'T EVEN GO THERE

"See, I am doing a new thing! Now it springs up; do you not perceive it? I am making a way in the desert and streams in the wasteland."

(Isaiah 43:19 – NIV)

Hallelujah – I am now walking in my purpose and fulfilling my God-ordained destiny. Who would have thought that I, Patricia Schelioaas Hatcher-Jones, would be used by God to help others? Certainly not me, considering my rough journey and late start. Reflecting on my preteen and adolescent years, I can only thank my Heavenly Father for keeping His hand upon me. Today, as a woman being used by God in Ministry, I know I have a victorious testimony only by God's grace. My journey to this point has been filled with detours and dead ends. I took so many wrong turns and visited some unfriendly territories. So many times, I heard these words ringing in my ear with urgency – "Uh-uh, daughter, don't even go there!"

1

Unfortunately, I didn't heed the warning in many circumstances, and consequently, I suffered greatly.

This is my story. I was the fifth of six children born to Ray and Mildred Hatcher. I didn't have any biological sisters. It was tough growing up with all brothers. I often wished that I had an older sister. Since I was the only daughter born to Mildred Hatcher, it was all trial and error when it came to rearing me. Mama was a professional woman. She graduated from an all-black Southern University and obtained her Masters and Counseling degrees. Mama was an activist and community leader. She had such compassion and passion for those who were considered underdogs. Mama came from a family of seven girls and one boy, the opposite of my family makeup. As a child, I didn't know that Mama's rearing decisions, when it came to me, her only daughter, were to help me, not hurt me.

My parents divorced when I was around 11 years old. This was a devastating time for me. They say, and I would have to admit, that I was my daddy's girl. Perhaps it was because I was my daddy's only girl. I adored my daddy. To me, he was the greatest, most loving, caring, and responsible man alive. Daddy took care of my ears when I got them pierced. It was Daddy who took care of my severely burned leg when I accidentally dropped the iron on it at the age of eight. It was Daddy who talked kindly to me when Mama yelled at me. Oh yes, my daddy was and will always be my hero. I didn't want to do anything to make my daddy angry with me.

When my parents announced that Daddy was moving out of the house, I couldn't accept it. I cried and cried for days. I had so much pain in my heart. Why was Daddy leaving? I wondered if there was anything that I could do to change his mind. As my parents had discussed, Daddy moved out of the house into his apartment. Of course, I didn't know the full details of the breakup. I only knew how I felt about him leaving…I was devastated. Reflecting, I realize that his departure from our home was the beginning of my downward journey. My time with Daddy dwindled to weekend visits and summer vacations. Consequently, his fatherly influence in rearing me dwindled as well.

My wayward years began when I entered middle school at 12 years old. I was a seventh grader who thought I knew it all. I started liking boys around this age, and my way of letting the boy know I liked him was by beating him up. I know this is not a nice characteristic for a girl, but I grew up with all brothers, as I mentioned before. I survived by acting or pretending to be tough. As I look back, I can now see clearly that Satan had set many attractively disguised traps intended to kill me, steal from me, and destroy me. Those traps came in the form of men, drugs, low self-esteem, rebellion, fads, and self-centeredness. As a product of being primarily raised by a single parent who was busy ensuring that my basic needs were met, I became a prime candidate for Satan's traps. Yet, despite all of Satan's attempts throughout my life, I heard the Holy Spirit tell me time and time again, "Uh-uh, daughter, don't even go there."

I only wish I knew then what I know now about the plans God had for me versus the traps Satan had set for me. I invite you, my little Sista, to travel with me as I reflect on some of the detours I took before arriving at this new place. I want to help you avoid some pitfalls that could hinder or delay your divine destiny. We'll travel to some of the areas that attempted to trap me or some people dear to me, and I'll share with you some biblical references and truths that can be used to either help you avoid the trap or help you get delivered from the trap. You will be given an opportunity to answer a personal question and say an affirmation of agreement with God. Use the note sheets to record your thoughts. I will offer a prayer on your behalf and proclaim God's Word that you, too, will receive the "new thing" God is offering you. I must warn you that I will be very candid in my transparency, especially in Chapter Seven, because I want to keep it real with you.

Although there may be an age difference between me and the reader of this book, I can assure you that my journey will bear some similarities to yours. You see, King Solomon, considered the wisest man born to human parents, said there is no new thing under the sun. "The thing that has been, it is that which shall be; and that which is done is that which shall be done; and there is no new thing under the sun." (Ecclesiastes 1:9 - KJV),

I pray that you will pay close attention to the words written and hear the loving voice of Jesus say to you – ***"Uh-uh, daughter, don't even go there!***

PRAYER:

"Speak, Lord, for Your daughter hears You. In Jesus' Name, I pray
– Amen."

CHAPTER ONE

DON'T ALLOW MAKEUP TO CREATE A DIFFERENT YOU

"...look not on her countenance...for the Lord sees not as man sees; for man looks on the outward appearance, but the Lord looks on the heart."

(1 Samuel 16:7 – KJV)

Cosmetics, better known as makeup, can be hazardous to the real you – *"Uh-uh, daughter, don't even go there!"* Most young ladies are too eager to begin wearing makeup. Some parents permit their daughters to wear makeup when they are 16 and younger. Makeup is just that – it makes us up. We look older than we are. We rush to grow up. Makeup, when applied properly, can enhance, but it also deceives. It is also addictive. The more you use, the more you'll want to use. You start using lip gloss, then progress to lipstick, then eye makeup, liner, mascara, and the thinning or thickening of your eyebrows. Then you graduate to face makeup, foundation, blush, powder, false eyelashes, and even colored eye contacts. Then, the natural beauty is gone, and you are transformed into another person. People, especially older males, see you in a different light. They don't see you as a young lady; they see you as someone mature and ready to experience womanly adventures.

Right before your eyes, the real you vanishes, and the made-up you takes over—the texture and condition of your skin changes in the worst way. The younger you start using it, the longer you'll have to use it. If you start at 16 years old or younger, by the time you reach the wonderful age of 40, you'll be so addicted to makeup that you won't want to be seen without it.

Today, I see myself in so many young girls who are in a hurry to grow up. My aunt, who is now deceased, gave me some words of wisdom when I was around 16 years old. She told me that if I was going to wear makeup, I had to take the time each night to cleanse my face. Well, being the lazy person that I was at the time, I immediately thought that was way too much work; therefore, I decided that I didn't need that face of makeup. I am so thankful for my aunt's words of wisdom and concern. Because of it, my natural face was preserved much longer than it would have been if I had started using makeup at 16.

"Uh-uh, daughter, don't even go there!" You don't need to wear makeup of any kind until it is necessary. So many girls have naturally beautiful faces. Yes, makeup does enhance our natural features, but we don't want to become so made up that our natural beauty is lost. Makeup is like many other addictive devices - it is hard to break the habit. We are deceived when we look in the mirror. The devil whispers in our ear something like this, "You don't look good; your face is ugly." The next thing we do is cake on the makeup because we think it makes us look good. But when others see us, those who recognize true beauty, they perceive us in a different light than what we believe we are projecting.

I met a young lady who I noticed had the makeup really caked on. I guessed that she was in her 30s. Each time I saw her, I noticed that she was putting more and more makeup on. An opportunity presented itself for me to talk to her. The Holy Spirit led me to tell her, in love, that she naturally didn't need makeup and that she was an attractive young lady. When she told me that she was only 20 years old, I was not surprised that she looked older, considering all the makeup painted on her face. I told her she didn't need the makeup and that if she didn't wear it, she would still be noticed by the young men. It may be because I was a female, but this young lady did not believe what I was saying to her. She said she didn't think she would look better without it because she had been wearing it since she was 14. That meant she had been wearing makeup for six years and looked at least ten years older.

But it wasn't a good look; it was a fake look. It was so evident that she was overly made up. No man could see the true beauty in her. The message she was giving was, "See me." I do not doubt that she was the topic of many conversations involving males and females. But the conversations would not have been edifying to her.

Don't buy the devil's bag of lies. He is truly out to kill, steal, and destroy. To enhance your natural beauty, apply some eye makeup sparingly. Use subtle lipstick. And let me say something about those nails. Most young ladies want long, fabulous nails. But many times, they can't afford the upkeep. Consequently, you see young ladies with half-polished and often chipped nails. The golden rule is that if you wear colored nail polish, you must have it totally on or off.

Don't have nails so long that the first thing people notice is your nails. In my opinion, young girls under 18 shouldn't wear tips. A manicure with subtle nail polish looks very nice on young ladies.

The bottom line, my Sista, is that you must not allow makeup to create a different you. Man looks on the outward appearance, but the Lord looks on the heart. Don't buy into the lie Satan has told you about your looks. Just look in the mirror and see the beauty that God sees in you.

PERSONAL QUESTION:

▶ What does being fearfully and wonderfully made mean to you?

MY AFFIRMATION:

"I affirm I will always heed the warnings to avoid the zone of false appearance. I will always endeavor to see the beauty within me. I will open my eyes to see myself as The Creator sees me - fearfully and wonderfully made in His image."

PRAYER:

"Heavenly and Gracious God, Who made us in the image of Yourself, I pray for Your daughter to heed your warning to not go to the zone of false appearance. Show Your daughter how You see her in the beauty of holiness. Open her eyes to see herself as You see her – fearfully and wonderfully made in Your image. In Jesus' Name, I pray -- Amen."

Uh-Uh, Daughter, Don't Even Go There®

Notes/Thoughts:

_____

_____

_____

_____

_____

_____

_____

_____

_____

_____

_____

_____

_____

_____

_____

_____

_____

_____

_____

_____

_____

_____

CHAPTER TWO

DON'T LET YOUR FLESH DICTATE WHAT YOU WEAR

"In like manner also, that women adorn themselves in modest apparel, with shamefacedness and sobriety…"

(1 Timothy 2:9 – KJV)

S cantily clad attire (inadequately clothed) leaves nothing to the imagination – ***"Uh-uh, daughter, don't even go there."*** Oh, my little Sistas, be careful how you advertise. There is something about us females that causes us to dress provocatively and seductively at times. Could it be that we are seeking attention? It is not always the attention of men that we want, either. Sometimes, we want other females to notice us. However, the way we get noticed is often not what we intended. There are some outfits that God is saying to us, "Uh-uh, daughter, don't even go there." Those outfits reveal the secret parts of our flesh, such as the breast, butt, upper thighs, and even our bellies. We must ask ourselves: what message am I trying to give? We wear shorts and dresses that are so short we can't even sit down without tugging or covering up with towels, scarves, or other items.

A man of quality doesn't want a woman or young lady who exploits herself for everyone to see. No, he is interested in the inner beauty. He is looking at how she carries herself and whether she respects herself. He is looking to see if she is loud or rather flamboyant. Usually, a young lady willing to reveal her secret parts to anyone looking is struggling with her self-image. If you want to know who you are, look at what you attract and how you attract. People are going to treat you like you treat yourself. Think about it. If you dress yourself in such a way that young men think they can grab and tug at you, that is exactly what will happen. A low self-image will cause you to stoop very low. You will begin to compromise what is righteous to the Lord. I was a teenager during the era when hot pants and sizzlers were the fad. Sizzlers were those micro-mini dresses that were so short they came with matching panties. But because this was the "in thing," I begged my mother to buy me a couple of the outfits, and she reluctantly did. I thought I had it going on. But I said, "Look at me; I got something you want."

I have always loved fashion. In my teens, halter tops, hot pants, lace pants, or whatever revealed the skin was hot, and I wore it. I had what some considered a cute shape, and I knew how to draw attention to it. My hair was always tight. I wore body art (fake tattoos), thinking I was doing it for me, but really, I was doing it to draw attention to me. There were times when I put on clothes, and I heard the voice of God say, "Uh-uh, daughter, don't even go there." But I ignored the voice and went there anyway. The result was that I drew the attention of men I wasn't interested in. I realized that some men would give up things to get what they wanted, which is sex. And since I was advertising that I had something to sell, they were willing to pay. Sounds cheap, doesn't it? I devalued myself by projecting a sexy image. My entire purpose for dressing provocatively was to get the attention of the young and not-so-young men. I thought that the men wanted someone who was sexy looking on the outside.

I caught exactly what my appearance advertised for – disrespectful bad boys and lustful men. I looked like I was easy, and I believe that if it had not been for my over-protective brothers, I would have found myself a victim of unwanted attention and or abuse -- in other words, rape or sexual assault.

You see, my Sista, our flesh will crave attention, and if we don't heed God's warning not to "go there," we can find ourselves in uncomfortable and disgraceful situations. I've discovered that a quality man wants and deserves a quality woman and that I can still look appealing without compromising the integrity of my character. To parade around in scantily clad clothing is to dress less than sufficient or less than quality. So, my Sista, since you are a person of quality, you should not allow your flesh to dictate what you wear.

PERSONAL QUESTION:

▶ What kind of self-image are you projecting with the outfits you wear?

MY AFFIRMATION:

"I affirm not to allow my flesh to dictate what I wear, especially if the goal is to intentionally reveal my body for attention. I will endeavor to display the quality and gift that I am in a manner that pleases my Creator. I will not yield to peer pressure. I will build my self-esteem in such a way that I will always know I am valuable."

PRAYER:

"Heavenly and Gracious God, Who made us in the image of Yourself, I pray for Your daughter to heed your warning not to allow her flesh to dictate what she wears, especially if the goal is to intentionally reveal her body for attention. Show Your daughter how to display the quality and gift that she is in a manner that pleases you. Protect her from the temptation of yielding to peer pressure. Build her self-esteem in such a way that she will always know that she is valuable to You. In Jesus Name, I pray - Amen."

Uh-Uh, Daughter, Don't Even Go There®

Notes/Thoughts:

_____

_____

_____

_____

_____

_____

_____

_____

_____

_____

_____

_____

_____

_____

_____

_____

_____

_____

_____

_____

_____

_____

_____

CHAPTER THREE

DON'T STEP OUTSIDE YOUR LANE "HE SAID, SHE SAID"

"A gossip betrays a confidence; so avoid a person who talks too much."

(Proverbs 20:19 – NIV)

"Let no corrupt communication proceed out of your mouth, but that which is good to the use of edifying, that it may minister grace unto the hearers."

(Ephesians 4:29 – KJV)

"He said, she said" is better known as gossip, and it can get you in a world of trouble – ***"Uh-uh, daughter, don't even go there!"*** Our mouths can get us in a heap of trouble if we're not careful. What is it about us that influences us to step outside our lane? You know -- getting involved in things that are none of our business, giving opinions that are evil-spirited, or repeating conversations about people behind their backs?

There is a danger of traveling outside of your lane. What I mean by this is there is a danger in getting into business that is not yours or involving yourself in other folks' business. I learned first-hand how gossiping can get you into trouble. One day, at a job I had been working for about three months, I overheard a supervisor talking negatively about one of her employees. I was offended by what she said and felt obligated to tell the person who she was talking about what she said. I guess I was oblivious to what she would do with the information. The next thing I knew, the supervisor had it in for me. She exercised all her privileges as a supervisor to make my working environment unbearable. She went to her supervisor and fabricated her side of the story. When she was finished, I was made to look like a troublemaker who wasn't cut out to do my work. Lies were told about me not being a good worker and that I sat around idle and did not do my work. My character was being assassinated right before my eyes. I was given a performance report that said I was a "needs improvement" employee with two months to improve my performance or be rejected from permanent working status. Needless to say, I was shocked by the accusations and very concerned about my working future. Not only did I receive a negative job performance report, but my salary step increase was denied, and I was denied approval for my scheduled vacation. To make matters worse, they changed my job assignment and required me to work in the mail and file room and report directly to the supervisor who was talking about the employee. My life was a living nightmare. At first, I responded in the flesh as most people would do, but then the wisdom of God came upon me, and I knew that I had to go into battle for the reputation of my character. Since I wasn't a permanent employee, I had no union representation, but I had my mama. Not only did my mama pray for me, but she gave me guidance on what I needed to do. I had to write a response to refute the accusations and punishment and formerly reject them as unfair treatment. Based on the procedures for grieving adverse employee action, I had three levels to appeal to. The first level was to my accuser's supervisor, who rejected my rebuttal because she was already in cahoots with the punishment. The next level was the Executive Director's level. Now, this is where the wisdom of God came in. Usually, the complaint is handled by the assistant executive director, who makes a recommendation to the executive director. However, I learned that the Assistant Executive Director was also in on the initial adverse action; therefore, he would most likely reject my rebuttal. I delivered my rebuttal to the Executive Director, who read it and scheduled a meeting with me. As I said, I didn't have union employee representation, so my mama accompanied me to the meeting. My mama was a certified school counselor, so she had some experience defending those who needed to be defended. After all the facts were presented, it became clear to the Executive Director that I had been treated unfairly. Ultimately, I didn't have to appeal to the third level because my salary increase was granted. My following job performance report was outstanding, I was given another job assignment, my vacation was approved, and I was granted permanent working status.

I traveled through the valley of death all because I got myself involved in something that was not my business. I became a partaker of gossip. The supervisor was not talking to me; I merely overheard her. When I went and told the other person, it was hearsay. I didn't even know the other person that well. I involved myself for no other reason than to stir up trouble. I didn't heed God's warning, "Uh-uh, daughter, don't even go there." We can so easily get mixed up in the drama that it can cause pain for others. When I told the person what I heard the other person say about her, her feelings were hurt. When I repeated the negative words, I caused pain. And then, when the other person found out what I had done, she was angry. So, I not only caused pain, but I also influenced anger. Neither was good. If I had stayed in my lane, I would have avoided sending others through anguish and sending myself down a path of heartache, embarrassment, opposition, and rejection.

No good thing comes out of gossip. Sometimes, it is hard not to involve ourselves in conversations that could have a negative impact on others. But the Word of God tells us to flee from the appearance of evil. To talk about others behind their backs is evil. We should practice keeping our mouths shut or praying about the situation and leaving it in God's hands. We tend to talk about others sometimes, I believe, to lift ourselves. However, it doesn't work because blowing out someone else's candle doesn't make our candle shine any brighter. But it could result in devastating pain to another person. If you don't have anything good to say, it behooves you not to say anything at all. If you hear something negative, don't repeat it. Just stay in your lane.

PERSONAL QUESTION:

▶ Are you in control of your tongue and the words you speak about other people?

MY AFFIRMATION:

"I am truly sorry for the times or time when I stepped outside of my lane and involved myself in conversations that were not my business. I affirm that I will not fall prey to the temptation of gossip or any other corrupt communication that would make me untrustworthy. I affirm I shall have victory over gossip and quarrels."

PRAYER:

"Supreme and Awesome God, we humbly come before You to ask for Your forgiveness for the time or times when we stepped outside of our lane and involved ourselves in conversations that did not please You. Your Word tells us that without gossip, a quarrel dies down. Please help Your daughter not to fall prey to the temptation of gossip or any other corrupt communication that You would consider untrustworthy. Thank You for the victory; in Jesus' Name, I pray – Amen."

Uh-Uh, Daughter, Don't Even Go There®

Notes/Thoughts:

_____

_____

_____

_____

_____

_____

_____

_____

_____

_____

_____

_____

_____

_____

_____

_____

_____

_____

_____

_____

_____

_____

_____

_____

CHAPTER FOUR

DON'T DEVELOP SHAKY RELATIONSHIPS

"Do not be unequally yoked together with unbelievers. For what fellowship has righteousness with lawlessness? And what communion has light with darkness?"

(2 Corinthians 6:14 – NKJV)

Unstable and insecure relationships will pull us down without knowing what happens – *"Uh-uh, daughter, don't even go there!"* Starting relationships can be easy, but maintaining relationships can be difficult. If our self-worth is only defined in a man's or woman's arms, we have been greatly fooled. We cannot snatch after any and everything and call it a relationship. If we seek anything else before God, it will be distorted and not firm. God has the key to our identity. Flesh and blood cannot define who we really are. Only God knows who we are. Pursuing relationships outside God's will could lead to destruction and despair. When we get involved with people we know are questionable, we'll prevent our friends, those who care about us, from meeting them. I once had a prayer partner, and we would call each other early in the morning for specific prayer. This young lady asked me to be her prayer partner, and I agreed. We would share personal challenges that we wanted to pray about, and after each prayer session, we truly felt that God heard our prayers and would move on our behalf.

Something occurred that caused us not to pray as often. Before I knew it, my friend had informed me that she had gotten married. I was shocked because she hadn't even mentioned that she had a man, let alone someone she was considering marrying. By accident, we ran into each other in public one day, and I had the opportunity to meet her husband. I immediately knew something was amidst and I could see why she didn't tell me about him. A few months later, she called me in distress and confessed that her husband was a drug addict and had influenced her to begin using drugs also…something she had been delivered from years ago. She was devastated. I was devastated but continued to pray for her. Unfortunately, the desire to stay in her unhealthy relationship with this man was stronger than her desire to be delivered. She eventually lost her job, her home, her friends, her dignity, and her relationship. My friend allowed God to slip to the back of the line. My friend knew she was accountable as long as we prayed together, and God would speak. But when she decided to no longer seek God, she opened herself up for Satan to attack fiercely. It took her a few years, but she found her way back to God and is determined to do things His way. But she would be the first to admit that before she made the dreadful mistake of pursuing a relationship with this man, she heard the voice of God say, "Uh-uh, daughter, don't even go there!"

What is it that causes us to navigate to unhealthy relationships? Could we so desperately want to love and be loved that we become totally blinded to all the "red flags" and deaf to the voice of God saying, "Uh-uh, daughter, don't even go there"? We pursue relationships without first having a solid relationship with the One Who knows us better than any other will ever know us. I suggest that we first turn our eyes upon Jesus.

In case you didn't know, Christianity comes out of a personal relationship with the person Jesus. Jesus is the Vine, and we are the branches connected to that Vine. The purpose of a branch is to carry all the characteristics of the vine inside of it. Jesus says, "Abide in Me." This means to abide in the person of Jesus, not just the salvation plan. To have and maintain that intimate personal relationship with Jesus, Christians have God's Holy Spirit (John 14:16).

We need to ask ourselves some point-blank questions -- how do I relate to people? How do I handle it when someone criticizes me? How do I handle it when someone spreads a rumor about me? How do I handle it when my best friend wants to spend time with their other friends? How do I handle it when I am being pressured by someone to compromise my commitment to Christ? And finally, if Jesus gave me a nickname that would pinpoint my dominant characteristic, what nickname would He give me?

If our honest response to any of the above questions is negative, we need to check our relationship with Christ. Without a solid relationship with the Lord, we are prone to seek someone else to love and define us. But when we seek Jesus, we are always loved and filled with God's Spirit. We're of a Royal Priesthood, too royal to enter into just any kind of relationship. We must know who we are and, more importantly, Whose we are. Low or no self-esteem will enable us to stoop low. We will compromise what is righteous to the Lord. For example, we might find ourselves in an intimate relationship where physical, emotional, and or sexual abuse exists. And the worst part about it is that we blame ourselves for the behavior of others. But we must allow God's Spirit to come out of our lives in how we relate to Him and the people around us. This is how we develop and maintain solid relationships.

My little Sista, if you are currently in a physically, sexually, or mentally abusive relationship, I've got good news for you. Today is your day to get out. Some of the signs include, but are not limited to, dominance, humiliation, isolation, threats, intimidation, blame, guilt, and violence. First, you must admit the truth about where you are. No more cover-ups, no more lies, and no more excuses. God has heard your cry, and He is saying it is time for you to come to Him right now. You can escape the abuse. You need to stop reading this book and get to a phone right now. Call the National Domestic Violence Hotline at

1-800-799-2233. Help is available 24 hours a day, 365 days a year. Do not allow shame, guilt, or fear to stop you from making the call. CALL NOW!

If you are in a shaky relationship that may not necessarily be abusive, but you know it is not right, choose to end it now and wait expectantly for God's best because you deserve it.

PERSONAL QUESTION:

▶ Do you seek approval from others through your relationship as a way to be accepted, even if it goes against your personal values? If so, why?

MY AFFIRMATION:

"I affirm I will develop healthy and solid relationships and not seek or enter into relationships that compromise my value. I affirm that I will endure and wait for relationships that add value rather than subtract from my life."

PRAYER:

"Sovereign and Holy Father, Who demonstrated Your love by sending Your Son Jesus to the cross so that we, Your creation, would be reconciled back in relationship with You, I ask You to help Your daughter develop healthy and solid relationships. I pray the Holy Spirit will lead her to a righteous relationship with Jesus and then to firm, uncompromising relationships with others. Help her to always seek relationships that please You, and give her the strength to wait on Your best. In Jesus' name, I pray - Amen."

Uh-Uh, Daughter, Don't Even Go There®

Notes/Thoughts:

CHAPTER FIVE

DON'T WASTE YOUR GREATEST ASSET, YOUR MIND

"My people are destroyed from lack of knowledge…"

(Hosea 4:6 – NIV)

D o not neglect the power of knowledge. The national slogan for the United Negro College Fund is "A mind is a terrible thing to waste." What a profound but true statement. If Satan had his way, we would all waste our greatest asset, which is our mind, by being slothful, lazy, and uneducated. Satan aims to fill our minds with waste, trash, vanity – anything that will distract us so he can destroy us. But God's voice constantly speaks to us and says, ***"Uh-uh, daughter, don't even go there."***

When I was in the seventh or eighth grade, one of my neighborhood friends, who was a few years older than me, told me how I could graduate from high school one year earlier than my regular schedule.

All I had to do was take extra classes during the regular school year, beginning in the 10th grade, and take summer classes. My mother promised to buy me a car when I graduated high school, so I had an incentive to finish school. What she didn't bank on was me finishing a year early. I took all the required courses, and I did, in fact, graduate one year earlier. I was 17 when I graduated. I didn't get the car upon graduation, but my mama fulfilled her promise and bought me the car a year later after turning 18.

Mama was an educator, so she naturally assumed I would follow in her footsteps. Although I was very focused on finishing high school one year earlier than I should have, I had no vision for my future. Mama helped me out a bit. She tapped into her connections and enrolled me at the local State University. I began my freshman year of college in the fall following my high school graduation. However, I was not prepared for college life. I didn't have a clue as to what I was doing. Since I lacked accountability, I went to class when and if I wanted to. I passed classes that I enjoyed and failed classes that I wasn't interested in. It was strange, but I didn't have a goal to finish school. I was not driven like I was when I was in high school. I didn't have any incentive to push me forward. I, however, was too wrapped up in myself…chasing behind boys that didn't add any value to my life.

So, when I was 19 years old, I decided that I didn't want to abide by Mama's house rules anymore, so I moved out of her house and moved in with my unfaithful boyfriend. He made it clear to me that I had to work. I learned very quickly and painfully that I couldn't depend on any man to take care of me. So, I tried attending school mainly to receive the grant money and work part-time. For a brief period, I made enough income to contribute to the cost of living with him, but I couldn't maintain my grades because I wasn't focused on school.

Consequently, I was put on probationary status, jeopardizing my grant money. After four years of staggering along, I eventually dropped out of college and found full-time employment. Mama was very disappointed because she had invested so much time and effort in pushing me forward, and she knew where I would be headed if I didn't get a college education. After two years of living with my cheating boyfriend, I decided that it was time for me to move out on my own. So, that is exactly what I did. I found a one-bedroom apartment and moved out. I loved my freedom, but I was the sole provider. I had to work to maintain my independent status.

Through the grace of God, I was blessed with good-paying jobs and could live comfortably. I obtained a permanent job with the State of California. I was a clerical, typing letters, answering phones, making deliveries, copying reports, etc. I performed the clerical functions for the professional analysts. One day, I was asked to make several copies of a report for an analyst. It was a thoughtless and annoying job. As I made the copies, I decided right then that I needed to return to school to become one of the analysts. And that is just what I did. I transferred to another department closer to the University and began pursuing my degree. This time I didn't have Mama to guide me and make connections for me. I researched what I needed to do and re-enrolled at the University. I was accepted and couldn't afford to fail any classes because I was footing the bill this time (there was no grant money to assist me). I changed my major a few times before realizing which major would be beneficial to my career growth. I ended up majoring in Public Administration. Because I worked full-time, I had to attend school part-time. I went to school all year and at night. I wouldn't get home until 11:00 p.m. after working all day and attending class. My weekends were filled with studying or being at school working on projects. My life was centered on school. But I was focused, and I was determined to succeed. It took me 9 years to get a BS degree, but I got it. It was one of the happiest days of my life when I received my diploma. I later returned and earned a master's degree in public policy and administration, which made my mama very proud.

When I left the old department before re-entering college, I remember saying that I would be back but would come back as an analyst. I didn't know it then, but I spoke prophetically because five years after graduating with my BS degree, I was hired at that same department as an analyst. The reason I was hired was because of my degree. I had taken the exam for an analyst. Thousands of people took the exam, but I scored in the first rank. Also, because I had a BS degree, I was contacted for an interview and offered the job.

I wasted so many years in college because I wasn't focused and didn't know how valuable education was to my future. If I had known what I learned when I was younger, I would have done things differently. When I was out of high school and in college, grant money was available to assist with the cost of my education. In addition, mama was willing to assist me. All I had to do was respect and obey her rules and do the work. But my vision was muddled; I had no long-term vision. I was confused, unsure, and very selfish. I let my flesh dictate what kind of future I would have. How silly I was. The voice of God shouted at me many times, "Uh-uh, daughter, don't even go there." But I didn't immediately listen. I traveled down my road, which came to a dead end, and I had to stop, make a U-turn, and travel back. My Sista, your greatest asset is your mind -- so don't waste it. Take advantage of every good opportunity to position you for increased knowledge and value.

PERSONAL QUESTION:

▶ What kind of information or thoughts do you feed to your mind?

MY AFFIRMATION:

"I affirm my mind will be stimulated so that my thoughts will always be pure and just and excellent. I affirm I will remain determined to reach my highest potential. I will rebuke any thoughts that would cause me to settle for mediocrity."

PRAYER:

"Gracious and loving God, the Giver of good and perfect gifts, thank You for being our mind regulator. I ask that You stimulate the mind of Your daughter in such a way that her thoughts will always be pure and just and excellent. Stir up within her the determination to reach her highest potential. Rebuke any thoughts that would cause her to settle for mediocrity. In Jesus' name, I pray – Amen."

Uh-Uh, Daughter, Don't Even Go There®

Notes/Thoughts:

_____

_____

_____

_____

_____

_____

_____

_____

_____

_____

_____

_____

_____

_____

_____

_____

_____

_____

_____

_____

_____

_____

_____

_____

CHAPTER SIX

DON'T ENTER FALSE COMFORT ZONES (ALCOHOL AND DRUGS)

"Wine is a mocker, strong drink is a brawler, and whoever is led astray by it is not wise."

(Proverbs 20:1 – NKJV)

"Be very careful, then, how you live—not as unwise but as wise, making the most of every opportunity, because the days are evil. Therefore do not be foolish, but understand what the Lord's will is. Do not get drunk on wine, which leads to debauchery. Instead, be filled with the Spirit."

(Ephesians 5:15-18 – NIV)

The definition of comfort is "to soothe in distress or sorrow; to ease the misery or grief, to bring consolation or hope to; and to give a sense of ease to." Loneliness, sorrow, disappointment, rejection, abandonment, fear, and crisis may lead us to seek comfort from various means. Some people try to find comfort in, to name a few things, alcohol, drugs, cigarettes, pornography, sex, shopping, eating, deceiving others, and excessive working. However, the sweet voice of God is saying, *"Uh-uh, daughter, don't even go there."* These comfort zones are false and may temporarily relieve our cravings, but they will not address the root problem. In fact, these false zones can often cause more agony and anguish than comfort.

As a child, I grew up around alcohol, and as a teen and young adult, I was around drugs frequently. I started smoking cigarettes openly at the age of 16, mainly because everybody else was doing it. My daddy acknowledges that he is a former alcoholic, and for most of my childhood years, up until my late 20s, I do remember seeing him drink a lot. It was common practice for my family to have lots of alcohol at family gatherings. My mother's side of the family loved to party, and their beverage of choice was the best alcohol their money could buy.

Consequently, my brothers and I were exposed to the availability and influence of alcohol throughout our formative years. I remember being at family barbeques, and while the adults drank and played cards, we, the children, would sneak and basically steal cigarettes and alcohol and then go and have our private parties. Of course, we knew what we were doing would not have been approved by our parents, but we honestly didn't see any harm in indulging. It became common for us to consume the substances because we wanted to feel good like everybody else.

I started first by smoking cigarettes. I thought smoking presented me in a very cool fashion. I even had a very sophisticated-looking cigarette case for the sole purpose of impressing others. As I said, I started smoking openly, meaning I didn't try to hide it from my mama when I turned 16 years old because that is when my brothers were allowed to smoke freely in front of my mama. There was a time when every member of my family smoked cigarettes -- none of us really enjoyed it. However, smoking cigarettes, as bad as they were for my health, was not the worse false comfort zone that I entered. One day, while visiting a friend who lived down the street from me, I was offered some alcohol. I can't remember exactly what I drank, but I remember so clearly that I drank it quickly, and not only did I get drunk, but I got sick as well. My friend's parents weren't home, but one of the oldest daughters was in charge. Of course, they panicked because of my intoxicated condition, but they were able to get me sober and returned home without my mama ever finding out about the situation until...

I accompanied my mama to a party one of her cousins was giving. I was still under the age of 21, but without my mama's knowledge, I ordered a rum and cola drink from the bartender. He knew that I was underage, but he prepared the drink for me anyway. I quickly consumed the drink and returned to the bar for another. I was a bit tipsy at that point, but I could see him mixing the drink. He filled my glass about three-quarters full of rum and topped it off with a bit of cola. I accepted the drink and once again consumed it very quickly. What I hadn't done was fill my stomach with food, so I quickly transitioned from having a buzz to becoming drunk, and boy, did I embarrass my mama. I threw up all over the kitchen floor causing my mama to clean up after me. I ruined her good time because she had to spend the rest of the evening caring for me. Of course, my mama was disappointed, but she still showed me a level of compassion until one of my brothers revealed to her that I had gotten drunk and sick before at my friend's house -- so much for brothers keeping a secret for you. Mama was furious with me and told me so in her mama way.

Unfortunately, I didn't learn my lesson from either of those incidents. I got drunk and sick a few more times before I realized that I didn't like drinking. But then drugs became my zone of choice. As I mentioned before, I was exposed to drugs frequently. I never had a problem getting access to them. Often, I was offered drugs like it was candy. Usually, it was because a male was trying to get next to me or because he indulged, and I followed suit because I was hanging with him. Many times, I got high on drugs just because my so-called friends were doing it, and I wanted so desperately to fit in and be accepted by them. I even did some very foolish things like smuggling marijuana in my suitcase and traveling from Hawaii to California -- not even thinking about the consequences of such stupidity. I also remember working at a military base and driving around with joints (rolled marijuana) in my ashtray until my boyfriend, who was a military policeman, told me what could happen to me if I were caught with the stuff.

After traveling down this road of destruction for several years, I began questioning myself as to why I was indulging in those substances that were creating false comfort zones. I didn't like drinking, so why did I drink? I didn't like smoking cigarettes, so why did I smoke? I didn't like doing drugs, so why did I do drugs? I finally concluded that I sought comfort in all these false zones. I considered when I indulged and discovered that sometimes I would consume to coat my emotional pain. Other times, I would consume to escape my painful reality. Many times, I consumed just for the heck of it. It boiled down to the fact that I was trying to find fulfillment in each of those substances but never was totally satisfied. Oh, I experienced a temporary escape, but it was just that – temporary. And yes, many times before I indulged, I heard those words, "Uh-uh, daughter, don't even go there." Unfortunately, I went there anyway. All of my brothers battled with addiction to alcohol, drugs, even gambling. This made me realize that it could have been me strung out fighting for recovery, but because of God's grace, I didn't become addicted, strung out, or brain-damaged during the process. Instead, I found my way out of the trap that Satan had so cleverly set for me.

Just before Jesus completed His assignment on earth, He told the disciples that He had to leave but that the Father (God) would send another comforter (the Holy Spirit) to abide with them forever (John

14:16). It is clear that Jesus knew that at some point during our lifetime, we would need to be comforted. Sometimes, God will use a human vessel to extend comfort to His children. But He would never use anyone or anything to replace what only He can provide.

When looking for comfort, we must turn to the True Zone for God's supply. We can find comfort in prayer, the Word of God, listening to the Word of God ministered through song, or just being still and listening to the Holy Spirit. God will never leave us or forsake us. Only God can provide us with an everlasting comfort zone. So, my Sista, before you consider entering a false comfort zone, "Uh-uh, don't even go there." Instead, turn to the Word of God and discover the True Comfort. If you are currently struggling with any substance, please seek help for deliverance from a qualified professional. You can also contact your local Alcoholics Anonymous or go to www.aa.org for related information.

PERSONAL QUESTION:

▶ What is your view about the effects of alcohol and drug usage?

MY AFFIRMATION:

"I affirm to cast down strongholds of any substance that would veer me into a false comfort zone. I affirm that I will not connect myself with anything or anybody that would lure me into entrapment. I affirm that I will pursue the necessary resources to strengthen myself from yielding to the temptations of seeking temporary relief from the false comfort zones."

PRAYER:

"Holy, Righteous, and Merciful God, I come before You on behalf of Your daughter, requesting that You anoint her with the power that destroys every yoke. I cast down the strongholds of any substance that is veering her into a false comfort zone. I ask that You fill her with Your Holy Spirit so there will not be room for an invasion of anything that is not of You. And if Your daughter finds herself in a false comfort zone, I'm asking that You immediately set her free from the entrapment and give her the strength to seek after Your comfort only. I praise You for the victory. In Jesus' name, I pray – Amen."

Uh-Uh, Daughter, Don't Even Go There®

Notes/Thoughts:

_____

_____

_____

_____

_____

_____

_____

_____

_____

_____

_____

_____

_____

_____

_____

_____

_____

_____

_____

_____

_____

_____

CHAPTER SEVEN

DON'T PARTAKE OF FORBIDDEN FRUIT (PREMARITAL SEX)

"But just as He who called you is holy, so be holy in all you do; for it is written: Be holy, because I am holy."

(1 Peter 1:15-16 – NIV)

"Don't you know that you yourselves are God's temple and that God's Spirit lives in you? If anyone destroys God's temple, God will destroy him; for God's temple is sacred, and you are that temple."

(1 Corinthians 3:16-17 – NIV)

Unfortunately, the best advice my mama gave me regarding sex, she thought, was that I needed to use birth control pills. Mama never talked to me about remaining a virgin until I married. As a young girl, I wasn't fortunate enough to hear about the "abstinent" campaign. Everybody my age was doing it, so I didn't feel remorse about trying it. But God's expectation was revealed in His words: ***"Uh-uh,***

daughter, don't even go there!" Unfortunately, once again, I did not heed His warning.

I lost my virginity at the age of 17. It was just something I thought was natural. I knew our bodies started moving in rhythm when I kissed my boyfriend. We would intensely engage with our clothes on that our bodies would get sore. The next level was destined to happen. He set things up for me. He took me to a place where we would not be disturbed. My boyfriend's stepfather had a second house he stayed in when he wanted to get away from his family. It was fully furnished, with all the comforts of home, and there we were with no intrusions…just me and my boyfriend. We had alcohol and weed (marijuana) –He was a little older than I was, but we were both under the age of 21. Of course, we had very sensual music. The atmosphere was perfect for sex, and we began our sexual encounter. First, the kissing started, then it intensified, and then the clothes came off. Our moment had come. The moment I had imagined so often. Nobody told me that it would hurt so much. I couldn't relax, and it was not a pleasurable experience at all. Although my boyfriend was experienced at having sex, he never did get his groove on with me because I could not relax. As I now reflect on that encounter, I realize God did not intend for me to enjoy the forbidden fruit. That first sexual experience was a complete disaster. I later broke up with that boyfriend, but not before making a couple of more unsuccessful attempts to have sex with him.

Satan, however, didn't stop there. A stranger came to town. I was so young and naïve. At 19, I met a young man three years older than me. He had just been discharged from the Army and wasn't a native of my hometown. Nobody knew him in my neighborhood, so I thought I had someone special. To top it off, he was a musician who played his instrument with much sex appeal. Little did I know that I was being set up once again by Satan for a great fall.

This brother was fine, and he knew what to say to turn me on. I was so drawn to him, especially when I saw how jealous the other guys in my neighborhood were because he had me, and they didn't. One guy who liked me tried to pick a fight with him. I was scared for my new boyfriend, but I was also flattered by the false attention. I threw myself at this man by yielding to his every beck and call. He taught me about sex in ways that blew me away. I experienced my first orgasm with him, and he introduced me to oral sex. Although it was something I considered repulsive, I indulged in it because I wanted to please him. Every time we were together, we had sex, and it didn't matter where.

I became aware that my new boyfriend was addicted to sex. He took me to X-rated drive-in theaters, and of course, we had sex in the car. Although his sex drive was sickening to me, I continued to want him. I saw him as my ticket out of my mama's house. So, after about six months of sleeping with him, I moved in with him. He didn't invite me, but I couldn't continue getting away with coming home at 2:00 and 3:00 in the morning. Mama wasn't putting up with it. So, there I was, totally out of the will of God and disappointing my daddy because I was shacking up with a man who wasn't my husband. And the saddest thing about it was that I didn't even think about marrying him. He was a whoremonger, and he cheated on me repeatedly. This man tried to totally crush me, but I was in a trap, and I didn't think I had a way of escape.

Oddly though, amid all my mess, I still heard the faint voice of God say, "Uh-uh, daughter, don't even go there." I later realized that my mama and daddy never stopped praying for me. After two years of living in that sinful manner, I gained enough strength, courage, and wisdom to move out on my own. Unfortunately, I didn't escape from my trap without deep wounds.

The choices we make today can have dire consequences tomorrow. Before I committed my life to Jesus, I dated a young man who was a native of another Country. He was a pleasant man who treated me well. I entered a sexual relationship with him, which lasted about six months. After I realized he was not the one I would marry, I cordially ended the relationship.

About six years later, I was faced with the opportunity to donate blood. I very proudly signed up to give blood. During the screening process, I was asked several personal questions. One of the questions that I was asked was if, within the past 20 years, I had had sexual intercourse with anyone from the particular part of the Country that my ex-boyfriend was from. I had to give an honest answer, so of course, I said yes, but I tried to explain that he always used a condom. My explanation was not good enough. I was rejected from giving blood because they could not take the risk.

I left the clinic feeling ashamed and humiliated. How could my behavior of the past have a bearing on what I was trying to do as a committed Christian woman? Oh, I thought, if only I could turn back the hands of time, I would not have entered into a sexual relationship with this man or any other man who wasn't my husband. I learned a very valuable lesson. There at that particular time of my life, this guy was nowhere in my life, yet my decision to go down that sexually active road resulted in me not being able to bless others with something I thought I could give, which was blood. I thank God that He shielded me from catching a life-threatening disease.

Before I yielded to the pressure of self-pleasure, I should have considered the long-term consequences, such as – pregnancy, sexually transmitted diseases, or even death.

My out-of-wedlock sexual encounters also resulted in two unplanned pregnancies that did not manifest life. When I got pregnant for the first time by my sex-addicted boyfriend, I couldn't even envision myself as being a mother at the age of 19. My first consideration, without reservation, was to have an abortion. It was an easy decision for me to make. I did it without thought. Nobody, other than who I confided in, knew about my dilemma. Oh, what a horrible mistake I made in aborting that child. Even today, I think about what I did and how wrong it was of me to take a precious life…a gift from God. I often think about who my child could have been. What right did I have to end the life within me? Although I know that I have been forgiven for my sin, I still have the memory that will be with me until the day I physically die.

My second pregnancy occurred when I was much older and truly knew better than to walk into the trap. I was very much involved in church, and yet I fell into sexual sin with someone I didn't even like. I gave into loneliness and yielded to the flesh. Consequently, I became pregnant. I knew that I could not abort the baby. When I told the Christian Brother that I was carrying his child, he abandoned me, and he totally rejected me. I encountered one of the most painful experiences of my lifetime. What was I to do? I felt I couldn't share my problems with others because of my fear of being judged. I cried out to the Lord and He comforted me. And the scripture He gave me via one of His servants was Isaiah 50:7-9 (NKJV), which says, "For the Lord GOD will help Me; Therefore, I will not be disgraced; Therefore I have set My face like a flint, And I know that I will not be ashamed. 8 He is near who justifies Me; Who will contend with Me? Let us stand together. Who is My adversary? Let him come near Me. 9 Surely the Lord GOD will help Me; Who is he who will condemn

Me? Indeed they will all grow old like a garment; The moth will eat them up."

I had decided to resign from all my church leadership positions and tell my family that I would be having a fatherless child. But I didn't get the opportunity to do either because three and a half months into the pregnancy, I had a miscarriage. It was another devastating time for me. What had happened, I wondered? Did my distress cause the miscarriage, or did God allow it to prevent a worse tragedy from occurring? Only God knows.

Less than a year after my miscarriage, God delivered me from my struggle with sexual sin. I purposed in my heart that the next man that I would have sex with would be my husband. God gave me a new life. He delivered me from all the memories of the past. He told me that He would keep me pure if I allowed Him to do so. However, I had to change my behavior patterns. There were things I couldn't do and places I couldn't go. I couldn't let men visit me late at night. I couldn't let them kiss or touch me. I couldn't listen to sensual music. I couldn't drink alcohol, which was a stimulant. I couldn't look at movies, videos or read books with sexual overtones.

Now I know that this probably sounds very extreme, but I had to heed to the Word that says, "Abstain from all appearance of evil." (1 Thessalonians 5:22). I had to continuously ask God to strengthen me and ask the Holy Spirit to keep me. Each day that I succeeded in walking in obedience, my strength was renewed. Satan, my enemy, tried to send one last arrow my way in terms of sexual temptation, but my faithful God shouted those meaningful words to me, "Uh-uh, daughter, don't even go there!" This time, I heard and obeyed Him!

Nearly six years after being delivered from my sexual struggle, I was married and made love for the first time to my husband on our wedding night. It was a blessed and ordained time.

If you are unmarried and have never been married before, to be able to say you are a virgin, whether male or female, is a badge you should be honored to wear. Virginity, in today's world, appears to be taboo. Yet, to be included in the number is so special. You can never go back to being a virgin. If you're sexually active outside of marriage, you can stop and abstain from sex until you're married, but you still can never truthfully say you're a virgin.

If you're a Christian, you've been blood washed. You are of Royalty. Tell Satan to back off and get his hands off royalty. You're Holy, so live Holy. Young ladies, you don't have to yield to sex to prove to a young man that you are a woman or that you are with it. Sexual activity doesn't define you as a woman. Falling into sexual sin happens because it is easier at the moment – we just get caught up in the moment. However, that moment of pleasure or pain, as in my case, can result in a lifetime of agony, so don't partake of the forbidden fruit.

PERSONAL QUESTION:

▶ What is your opinion about premarital sex?

MY AFFIRMATION:

"I affirm to exercise wisdom and strength to avoid yielding to the urges of my flesh. I affirm to live holy, righteous, moral, and pure. I affirm and actively pursue strategies for conquering the temptations of lust. I affirm to guard my eyes and ears from receiving anything unholy."

PRAYER:

"Most Heavenly and Gracious God, we thank You for keeping us from falling and presenting us before Your throne faultless. We know that it is Your command that we live holy as You are Holy, but we need Your help. I ask that You give Your daughter wisdom and strength to avoid yielding to the urges of her flesh. Show her how to live holy and righteous before You. Cleanse her from fleshly thoughts that could lead her to acts of immoral behavior. Reveal to her strategies for conquering temptations of lust. Guard her eyes and ears from receiving anything unholy and forbidden in Your sight. In Jesus' name, I pray – Amen."

Uh-Uh, Daughter, Don't Even Go There®

Notes/Thoughts:

_____

_____

_____

_____

_____

_____

_____

_____

_____

_____

_____

_____

_____

_____

_____

_____

_____

_____

_____

_____

_____

_____

CHAPTER EIGHT

DON'T FAIL TO HONOR YOUR PARENTS

"Honor your father and your mother, as the LORD your God has commanded you, that your days may be long, and that it may be well with you in the land which the LORD your God is giving you."

(Deuteronomy 5:16 – NKJV)

Perhaps you're like me and struggled with having a good relationship with your mother. I was a daddy's girl, so my relationship with him was great. But mom…that was a different story. I rebelled greatly against my mama, and God constantly warned me, ***"Uh-uh, daughter, don't even go there."*** From the time I was an adolescent until I was a young adult, I thought my mother didn't like me. She often said things, I thought, to hurt me deliberately. She accused me of doing things I did not do and, at times, talked to me like she didn't like me. Of course, I blamed her for it all. I developed such a bad attitude towards my mama, and all I could think about doing was getting out of her house as soon as I was legally able to do so. I can shamefully admit that there were times my mama made me so mad that I would cuss at her and say some hateful things to her. After I began seeking a relationship with Jesus, my heart towards my mama began to change. I became more sensitive to her and started gaining an understanding of her character. I realized that my mama tried her best to prevent me from traveling down the destructive road she had traveled, and how she went about it was the best way she knew how.

One day, out of the blue, my mama revealed to me that a couple of men physically abused her in her past. She was beaten almost to death. Mama told me she went after men with nice cars because she thought they had money. But she said she paid a great price for being with those men. Mama told me that she didn't want me to make the same mistakes that she had made, so she did whatever she thought she could do to prevent that from happening. Sometimes, that meant telling me I couldn't go somewhere or have something I wanted. Sometimes, that meant accusing me of having sex when I was way too young to be even thinking about it. Sometimes, that meant taking me to the doctor to have me examined and given birth control pills even if I wasn't having sex and was embarrassed because of the insinuation. In my view, mama's parenting skills were horrible. But my mama loved me, and she invested in me to a great extent. As I got older, I realized how much time, energy, and resources my mama poured into me. She paid for me to take dance classes. She involved me in the Girl Scouts. She made sure that I was involved in civic and community organizations.

She helped me get enrolled and accepted into college. She made sure that I was a debutant and presented to society even when I didn't know what the heck I was doing.

I eventually matured into a great love and appreciation for my mama. As God would have it, the script was flipped on me. I bought my first house down the street from where my mama lived. Mind you, when I moved away from Mama's house at 19, I tried to get as far away from her as possible. However, an opportunity was presented to me to buy a home, which I later came to acknowledge was a setup by God. When purchasing the house, I didn't know I would need to be close to Mama because she would need me. God taught me patience through my mama. God taught me forgiveness through my mama. Through my mama, God taught me how to give unconditional love. Mama was diagnosed with dementia, which is a form of Alzheimer's, and for the last seven years of her life, I was constantly involved with her. She lived with me for the last 13 months of her life, and I was so grateful to God that He allowed me to show Mama my appreciation for the great investment she imparted in my life.

Although there were times when I dishonored my mama in countless ways, God allowed me to repent and get it right. I was so blessed to have my mama as my mama. She was a wonderful woman who did her best with what she had. To honor means to respect. God commanded that we honor our parents. We may not like what they say, what they do, or how they act. But that doesn't really matter. What matters is what God expects from us. It is amazing how when I matured in my relationship with the Lord, He would guide me to pray for my mama rather than fuss at my mama. What a difference this act of obedience made. God answered prayer in so many ways and at so many times.

Some may have a solid relationship with their mama but a broken or non-existent relationship with their daddy. Maybe you feel abandoned or even rejected by your absentee parent, and your natural instinct is to disrespect them with nasty words or a bad attitude. Although your experience may be heartbreaking, I believe that you have the power to overcome the feelings of despair. Honoring our parents is the right thing to do and is mandatory. My Sista, don't fail to honor your parents; after all, if not for them, there would be no you.

PERSONAL QUESTION:

▶ What kind of expectations do you have from your parents?

MY AFFIRMATION:

"I affirm I will honor my parent and those in authority over me. I affirm I will ask for forgiveness for any acts of disobedience or dishonor I have made. I affirm that I seek understanding when I disagree with decisions made by my parent(s) or those in authority over me. I affirm I will endeavor to love unconditionally."

PRAYER:

"Our Heavenly Father Who is Supreme above all, we thank You for the gift of parents. In Your sovereignty, You gave us the parent or parents we had, whether biological, adoptive, court-appointed, or spiritual. Teach Your daughter how to honor her parent or parents in all her ways. Reveal Yourself to Your daughter as the ultimate parent so she can see why You designed this order. Please forgive any acts of disobedience and or dishonor made by Your daughter. Give Your daughter understanding when she disagrees with her parent's decision and show her how to love unconditionally. In Jesus' name, I pray – Amen."

Uh-Uh, Daughter, Don't Even Go There®

Notes/Thoughts:

_____

_____

_____

_____

_____

_____

_____

_____

_____

_____

_____

_____

_____

_____

_____

_____

_____

_____

_____

_____

CHAPTER NINE

DON'T LIVE WITH UNFORGIVENESS

"For if you forgive men when they sin against you, your heavenly Father will also forgive you. But if you do not forgive men their sins, your Father will not forgive your sins."

(Matthew 6:14-15 – NIV)

When we live in unforgiveness, the person we hurt is self, so, *"Uh-uh, daughter, don't even go there."* Forgiving those who trespass against us is not always easy. Our memory of the betrayal oftentimes resurfaces and opens old wounds. Sometimes, an unforgiving spirit hovers over us, influencing our thoughts and actions. Not only does God command us to forgive seventy times seven, but He also wants us to forget as well – putting those things behind us... God is a gracious God. He wouldn't place a commandment on us without providing us with the ability to obey. As we encounter the many circumstances that may cause us not to want to forgive someone for offending, hurting, disappointing, misusing, deceiving, or betraying us, we must seek God's Word to help us be obedient to Him. When we follow in God's manner, the blessings will flow, we'll experience overflow, and we'll have something to impart to others.

To forgive is to stop being angry about or resenting somebody or somebody's behavior. It means to pardon somebody for a mistake, misunderstanding, wrongdoing, or inappropriate behavior. In essence, it means to cancel an obligation such as a debt. When we are offended by someone and develop an unforgiving heart, we give that person power over us. Unforgiveness births bitterness, hurt, anger, resentment, frustration, depression, and even sickness.

There have been a few occasions when I have been betrayed by people I thought should have been more trustworthy. I recall one of my friends who deliberately started messing with my ex-boyfriend just to hurt me. He was someone I hadn't seen in years, and when she saw him greet me, she knew he was still very fond of me. I was excited to see him. I wasn't interested in hooking back up with him; I was just happy to see how his lifestyle had transformed for the better. She saw how much our encounter pleased him, and I think that is when her plan to go after him went into action. What hurt me the most wasn't the fact that she pursued a relationship with him but that she did it to spite me. She and I disagreed about another issue, and I believe she was fueled with a spirit of revenge. She entered an ungodly relationship with the fellow, which got her in a heap of trouble. She found out that he was married, and unfortunately, she unintentionally got pregnant but chose to abort the baby. All this happened to her because she pursued a relationship out of spite. She informed me about her situation, including the fact that she betrayed me. She asked for my forgiveness and was genuinely remorseful. I was left with the choice of whether to forgive her and dismiss her from my life or retain a relationship with her. I realized that although she intended to hurt me, she was the one who was in greater pain. The moment of her pleasure turned out to be a lifetime of bad memories and regret. It took the Spirit of God within me to forgive her and be a true friend during her great times of need. I had to look beyond myself and the hurt of being betrayed to see her greater need. We maintain a friendship to this day, and I believe we have become better women because of the experience. Forgiveness is not only the right thing to do but is also very liberating and empowering.

Another situation I experienced that required me to forgive and let go involved another guy. This time, however, he was the one who betrayed me. I was engaged to be married to a charmer. He was fine and kind. As we got closer to our wedding date, I began feeling less sure about whether I should marry him. Because we were both Christians, we decided together that we would abstain from having sex until we got married. I must be honest and say that we had already engaged in premarital sex before making our commitment to abstain. However, because we knew that fornication was not pleasing God, we committed to stop until we were married. About a month before our wedding day, we mutually agreed that we weren't ready for marriage and decided to postpone the wedding. We were still engaged, but we believed we needed more time to develop our relationship. Less than two weeks after our decision, I received a call from my fiancé's nephew informing me that he had just caught his girlfriend in bed with his uncle (my fiancé).

I found out that my fiancé had been having an affair with his nephew's girlfriend for some time. Needless to say, I was devastated and very angry. I wanted to inflict bodily and emotional pain upon him; I wanted him to suffer for the pain he inflicted upon me. After I cooled down, I realized that I wasn't the greatest victim in the situation. I didn't even have to see my ex-fiancé again, but his nephew was blood-related. Once again, through the strength of God, I could forgive my offender, set him free from the guilt, and free myself from the pain. He ended up marrying someone else, and ten years after our scheduled wedding, I married my husband.

When I was a young girl, I was repeatedly sexually violated by several male family members and neighbors. I never told anyone about any of my violations, and I erased the memory of the encounters from my mind until I attended a conference at a grown age where molestation issues were discussed. I never have confronted my offenders, and some of them have since died. I forgave them in my heart and endeavored not to allow their past behavior to have a hold on me. I don't know how they resolved their acts of violations with themself, but I know that I have been set free from any adverse effects. I genuinely pray those living secret offenders have worked out their forgiveness with God and themselves.

In all these incidents, I had a choice of whether to forgive or not. The offenses were real and caused me great pain. The easiest path for me would have been to totally dismiss these people from my life and avoid contact with them, but I wouldn't have been totally free. So, I chose to forgive. I forgave them, not just in words but in action. I didn't and still do not hold any grudges or blame against any of my past offenders. I've come to accept the encounters as part of my life-learning experiences. I freed myself from becoming a victim of bitterness and anger. I empowered myself to be victorious. To this day, I can see any of those individuals and genuinely treat them with love.

Indeed, during my lifetime, there have been many more offenses against me by others that have required me to forgive, and there will no doubt be others I have yet to face. I hear God saying that forgiving those who wrong us is mandatory and not an option. Satan would have us think that there are just some things that cannot be forgiven. Jesus says, "Uh-uh, daughter, don't even go there." Don't live in a state of unforgiveness. Don't let unforgiveness hinder you from growing to your fullest spiritual potential. If you expect to be forgiven for your transgressions against God, you must forgive those who have transgressed against you.

PERSONAL QUESTION:

▶ Do you realize how much forgiveness can be liberating and empowering for you?

MY AFFIRMATION:

"I affirm I will forgive those who have offended me in any way. I release anything that has weighed me down by another person's negative behavior or negative words towards me. I affirm that I seek strength to forgive my offenders. I refuse to give up my joy and peace. I affirm I will live in forgiveness."

PRAYER:

"Most Holy God, You reign in power and majesty above all circumstances. Thank You for providing Your Son, Jesus Christ, who opened the way for us to approach You with petitions and concerns. Right now, I pray that You will fill Your daughter with the desire to obey Your word as it pertains to forgiving those who have offended her in any way. Help Your daughter not to feel weighed down by another person's negative behavior or even her own. Please strengthen her to forgive. If joy has been robbed from her due to the offense, I ask that You restore the joy. Give her the ability to release all people and all situations into Your care. Please give her peace and a knowing that everything is already alright as she chooses to forgive those who have transgressed against her. Thank You for setting her free. In Jesus' name, I pray – Amen."

Uh-Uh, Daughter, Don't Even Go There®

Notes/Thoughts:

_____

_____

_____

_____

_____

_____

_____

_____

_____

_____

_____

_____

_____

_____

_____

_____

_____

_____

_____

_____

_____

_____

_____

_____

CHAPTER TEN

DON'T LET THE VOICE OF SUICIDE SPEAK

"This day I call heaven and earth as witnesses against you that I have set before you life and death, blessings and curses. Now choose life, so that you and your children may live; and that you may love the LORD your God, listen to his voice, and hold fast to him. For the LORD is your life, and he will give you many years in the land he swore to give to your fathers, Abraham, Isaac and Jacob."

Deuteronomy 30:19-20 (NIV)

The true enemy of our soul is none other than Satan. He desires to snuff out of us the very gift of life given to us by God Himself for a purpose. Satan's common strategy is to lure us into isolation -- meaning keeping us by ourselves -- so he can have our undivided attention and influence us to consider ending our lives. Suicide is defined as the act or an instance of intentionally killing oneself or the destruction or ruin of one's interests. Doesn't that sound just like what

Satan tries to get us to do at times? But the voice of God is speaking, *"Uh-uh, daughter, don't even go there."*

Satan cannot kill us, but what he can do is influence us into taking our own life. Think about that for a moment. In the Bible, there is a story about a man named Job. The Bible says that God told Satan that he could do a lot of things to Job, but he could not touch his life. During Job's trials and tribulations, and he had many, Job's friends thought he did something to deserve all his hardships. Even his wife thought he should just curse God and die. In other words, they tried to influence Job to take his own life. But Job chose life and declared, "All the days of my hard service, I will wait till my change comes." Job said, "Although I'm facing difficult days, I'll keep hoping and waiting for the final change." (Job 14:14 – NKJV) Job understood that his present circumstances, although very awful, were temporary and would change.

Death of our physical body is final; this we know. So why would we entertain making a final decision -- like ending our life -- based on temporary problems? One of the strongest tactics Satan uses against us is the spirit of fear. Fear is a spirit that is not of God. Yet, fear often grips us and births paranoia, depression, unreasonableness, confusion, and doubt. When we are in such a state of mind, we begin hearing Satan's voice louder than we can hear the voice of God, Whose plan is not to harm us.

The aftereffects of suicide are devastating to those who are left to live with the residue. I have had experiences with losing close friends and associates when they took their own lives. Leaving those of us who loved and cared for them searching for unanswerable questions. My first experience occurred when I was a teenager. One of my close friends in middle school took her life right before we were to graduate and move on to high school. Her actions left not only her family in a state of great grief but her peers as well. We just didn't have any understanding of why she would have made such a decision. She had so much purpose and potential. She listened to the wrong voice and chose to end her story.

I befriended a young lady who was going through some challenges in her life. She didn't give me the full details of her problems, but I could tell she was in a lot of pain. I prayed with her and encouraged her as best I could to keep trusting God. My faith told me that God would turn things around for her good. Within two weeks of our prayer, she took her life. Again, I witnessed someone who listened to the wrong voice and chose to end her story.

My friend's oldest grandson, who was 19 years old, handsome, outgoing, with a contagious smile and lots of potential for a successful life, experienced many challenges. It appeared that suddenly, the pressures of life overwhelmed him in the prime of his young adult life, and he decided to take his life because he listened to the wrong voice, thereby ending his story.

It was an early morning when I received a call from a friend who asked for prayer because she was being harassed and didn't feel comfortable living in her house. I arranged to visit her. Before leaving her home, I prayed with her, and when I left, she appeared to be empowered and encouraged. About a month later, I received another early morning call from her; her voice had the same urgency and concern. I initially prayed with her over the phone but had no peace afterwards. So, I went by her house and am so glad I did. At first, she appeared calm and ok. But after talking, I discerned she was having a great battle in her mind. Fear was the driving force, and she revealed to me that she was entertaining thoughts of suicide. Satan had already told her how to do it. But God used me to speak life by saying, "Uh-uh, daughter, don't even go there." We dealt with the spirit of suicide and fear right on the spot. We looked to the Word of God and got the ammunition we needed to muzzle Satan's voice. The Word of God says that perfect love, which comes from Almighty God, casts out fear. That is how we overcome the taunting voice of the enemy of our soul. My friend's story did not end because she decided to live and not die. Satan couldn't take her life, so he tried to get her to give her life up. As she began remembering the Word of God, she got stronger. God's voice became louder and clearer. She started feeling God's all-consuming love for her. She realized that God had a divine purpose for her, and she had not yet fulfilled her assignments in the land of the living.

I was once approached by a woman who informed me that her young adult daughter (a mother herself), who I did not personally know, was in the hospital after her third attempt to commit suicide. This disturbing information I received only a couple hours after receiving news that another young lady, who I did know, had successfully taken her own life. Needless to say, I was instantly moved to do whatever I could to prevent the young lady from ever wanting to attempt suicide again.

I made arrangements to visit her in the mental facility she had been admitted to. However, just as I reached the door to enter the facility, I suddenly realized I didn't know what to say to her. She didn't know me, I didn't know her, and I didn't want to risk saying the wrong thing to her. The voice of fear began speaking to me, saying, "What if you say the wrong thing, and who are you to say anything at all?" Then immediately, the voice of God spoke louder in my hearing and said, "You tell her, "Uh-uh, daughter, don't even go there. Tell her about My everlasting love for her and make sure that before you leave her presence, give her an opportunity to accept Jesus as her Savior." Her struggle with being loved was the root of this young lady's issue. She looked for love in all the wrong places, and when she failed to find it, she didn't think she was lovable and had anything to live for. Satan had influenced her to end her life by convincing her that nobody loved her. She had a beautiful daughter less than a year old, yet she didn't even see her daughter's love for her.

The young lady agreed to see me, and God used me as His vessel to speak to her about His everlasting love. I told her the truth about God's love for her and how His thoughts of her are many. I told her that she was fearfully and wonderfully made in the image of God. Then I told her that God had always loved her, and He always will love her, and that she had a divine purpose to fulfill in the land of the living.

Although extremely medicated, my young friend's mind was coherent long enough for her to hear the words God spoke to her through me. Before I left her, she accepted God's love and His Son Jesus as her Lord and Savior. The next time I saw her, she was at church with her daughter in tow, with a smile and a vision for her future. She chose not to end her story.

From a medical perspective, suicide can be triggered by depression or some other psychiatric disorders. Depression is not just a temporary mood, and it's not a sign of personal weakness. Depression is a serious condition with a variety of symptoms. Emotional symptoms can include sadness, loss of interest in things you once enjoyed, guilt or worthlessness, restlessness, and trouble concentrating or making decisions. Physical symptoms can include fatigue, lack of energy, and changes in weight or sleep patterns. Additional symptoms of depression may include irritability, anxiety, and thoughts of death or suicide. [1]

Many people suffer in silence with depression. Some are ashamed or afraid to seek help; others try to downplay the severity of their symptoms. It's important to remember that depression isn't something that's "all in your head."

Thoughts about death or suicide are common in depression, and it's important to take such thoughts seriously. If you feel like giving up or feeling as if you might hurt yourself, get help immediately: Call the National Suicide Prevention Helpline, 1-800-SUICIDE [1-800-784-2433] or 911.

God has given each of us the gift of free will -- meaning we get to make choices. We can choose to listen to His (God's) way, or we can choose to be deceived by Satan and go his way. God's path results in life and blessings, not death. Yes, there will be times when we will go through some valleys and experience some dark places; in essence, life will hit us hard. But when the voice of Satan begins to speak to us, we must remember the words that God is saying, "Uh-uh, daughter, don't even go there." We must listen to the voice of the One who covers us with His perfect love and desires that we choose life.

PERSONAL QUESTION:

▶ Do you know that God's love supersedes any troubling period you might be going through, and it's powerful enough to drive out all fear, depression, and anxiety?

MY AFFIRMATION:

"I affirm that I shall be an overcomer from bouts of depression, loneliness, and feelings of inadequacies. I affirm that I hold firmly to the truth about how valuable I am. I shall silence the voices that try to speak lies to me. I affirm I shall be an overcomer of any circumstance that tries to defeat me. I affirm that I will always choose to live."

PRAYER:

"Mighty God, the Lover of our soul, I come before You with appreciation for Your love for Your daughter. Thank You for her life and Your desire for her eternal life and abundant life. Please help her to overcome bouts of depression, loneliness, and feelings of inadequacy. Speak loudly in her ear about how valuable she is to You. Silence the voice of the enemy of her soul from speaking lies. Strengthen and equip Your daughter to overcome any circumstance that tries to defeat her. Always remind Your daughter of Your desire that she choose life and not death. In Jesus' name, I pray – Amen."[1]

---

[1] Information from www.cymbalta.com

Uh-Uh, Daughter, Don't Even Go There®

Notes/Thoughts:

_____

_____

_____

_____

_____

_____

_____

_____

_____

_____

_____

_____

_____

_____

_____

_____

_____

_____

_____

_____

_____

_____

_____

_____

TAKE HEED AND JUST DON'T GO THERE

"My sheep hear My voice, and I know them, and they follow Me."

(John 10:27 – NKJV)

Well, my Sista, what did you think about that journey? Some inescapable consequences can follow the wrong decisions we make. There are things we can do that we can never take back or recover from. For example, once we have sex, we can never again truthfully say that we are a virgin. Once we marry someone and divorce, we can never again truthfully say we've never been married. Once we have a child out of wedlock, we can never again say we have never had one out of wedlock. Once we take a smoke off a cigarette, or have a drink of alcohol, or a puff of marijuana, or a snort of cocaine, or a hit of crack, or a shot of heroin, or pop a non-prescribed pill, we can never again truthfully say we have never smoked a cigarette, drank alcohol, puffed marijuana, snorted coke, smoked crack, put drugs in our veins, or popped pills.

Contrary to popular belief, it is an honor to truthfully proclaim that we heeded the voice of God when He said, ***"Uh-uh, daughter, don't even go there!"*** God loves us more than we can comprehend. He knows the plans that He has for us. He will never set us up to harm or hurt us. His purpose for us is the best, and His ways are the best. If He warns us not to go there, then it would behoove us to obey and not argue.

If we have already gone "there," do not despair because God is a God of another chance. He is the Great Deliverer and a magnificent Sustainer. 1 Chronicles 7:14 says, if we repent and turn from our wicked way, God will forgive us and manifest healing (my paraphrase). So, whether you have just been thinking about "going there," you have "been there," or you're "there right now," be of good cheer because victory can be yours today – you need only to ask and obey. Get in alignment with God and allow Him to do a new thing in you!

PRAYER:

"Our Father Who is faithful and just on behalf of my Sista, Your daughter, I thank You for the lessons learned through life's experiences. Thank You for the wisdom and strength to choose the right direction. Thank You for the fresh perspective and the wealth of good that Your daughter has within. Thank You for never ceasing to speak truth to us. I pray that You will continue to order the steps of Your daughter, and may she find favor in Your sight. Fill her with wisdom, knowledge, understanding, discernment, and strength to avoid the pitfalls and traps that Satan has designed for her. Magnify Your voice in her ear so she can clearly hear Your warnings when You speak, "Uh-uh, daughter, don't even go there!" Thank You for the VICTORY. In Jesus' name, I pray – Amen."

Uh-Uh, Daughter, Don't Even Go There®

Notes/Thoughts:

_____

_____

_____

_____

_____

_____

_____

_____

_____

_____

_____

_____

_____

_____

_____

_____

_____

_____

_____

_____

_____

_____

_____

DISCUSSION QUESTIONS FOR FEMALE GROUPS

1. What usually makes you happy?

_____

_____

_____

_____

_____

2. What two things do you like about yourself? Why?

_____

_____

_____

_____

_____

3. What negative things have you thought about yourself? Why?

_____

_____

_____

_____

_____

4. What negative things have people said about you? How did it make you feel?

_____

_____

_____

_____

_____

5. What negative words have you spoken about another young lady? Why do you think you spoke those words?

_____

_____

_____

_____

_____

6. What positive things have you said about another young lady? What motivated you to speak those words?

    _____

    _____

    _____

    _____

    _____

7. What positive things have people said about you? How did their words make you feel?

    _____

    _____

    _____

    _____

    _____

8. When you see a young lady who perhaps is not dressed tastefully, and you're with your girls, what is your natural reaction?

    _____

    _____

    _____

    _____

    _____

9. Do you dress to impress others?

    _____

    _____

    _____

    _____

    _____

10. Who is your closest friend? Why?

    _____

    _____

    _____

    _____

    _____

11. Does your language vary depending on the company you're with? In other words, do you usually cuss around your friends or others that cuss?

    _____

    _____

    _____

    _____

    _____

12. Is there anyone who has offended you, but you haven't yet forgiven? If so, what is preventing you from forgiving?

_____

_____

_____

_____

_____

13. Is there anyone you need to ask for forgiveness from? If so, what is preventing you?

_____

_____

_____

_____

_____

14. What two things about yourself would you change if you could?

_____

_____

_____

_____

_____

15. If you could have one wish granted to you right now, what would it be and why?

_____

_____

_____

_____

_____

16. If there were no limitations, what would you like to do for the rest of your life?

_____

_____

_____

_____

_____

17. Do you have any regrets about the choices you have made so far during your life span? If so, what are they?

_____

_____

_____

_____

_____

18. If you could give someone a word of wisdom or advice, what would it be?

_____

_____

_____

_____

_____

19. Do you have a relationship with Jesus? If not, would you like to invite Him into your life now?

_____

_____

_____

_____

_____

20. Do you sometimes hear the voice of Jesus saying, "Uh-uh, daughter, don't even go there"? If so, what is your usual response?

_____

_____

_____

_____

_____

CONTACT AND CONNECT

Minister Patricia S. Hatcher-Jones

WEBSITE: www.linktr.ee/MzSchelioaas

EMAIL: LYBLE2020@gmail.com

Made in the USA
Las Vegas, NV
05 December 2024

13316751R00059